Please join us on Facebook

www.facebook.com/blissfulkidscoaching

blissfulkidscoaching@yahoo.com

All books can be found on Amazon and on our website

For more information visit www.patricia-may.com

Empower Kids Series

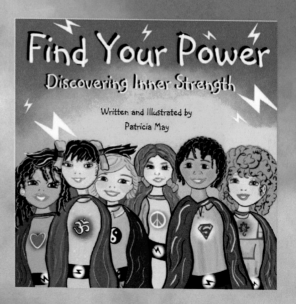

What Is Power?

Ask 10 people that question and most likely you will receive 10 deferent answers. The important thing is what power means to you. Within each and everyone of us, we carry our own personal inner power. When you are in balance with your own personal power, your capabilities are limitless, your desires are strong, your passion is forceful and your will is unstoppable! You are a superhero full of creativity and empowerment. Dreams are just the beginning of what is to come. It is the superhero within that no one but you has access to. For you and only you, have the power to create your own thoughts and desires.

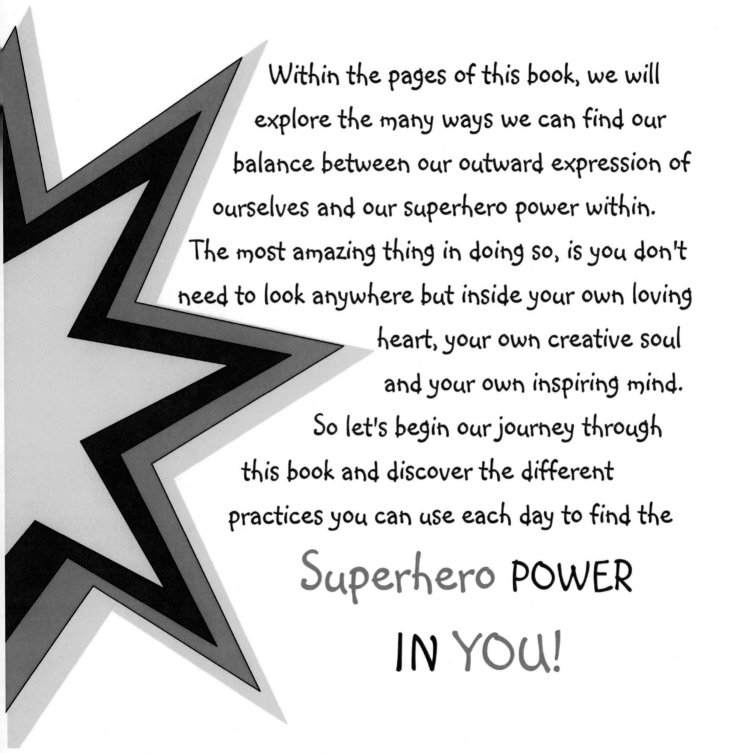

Within the pages of this book, we will explore the many ways we can find our balance between our outward expression of ourselves and our superhero power within.
The most amazing thing in doing so, is you don't need to look anywhere but inside your own loving heart, your own creative soul and your own inspiring mind.
So let's begin our journey through this book and discover the different practices you can use each day to find the

Superhero POWER

IN YOU!

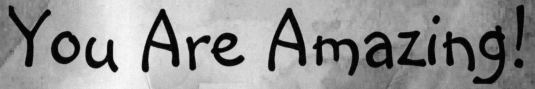

Celebrate You!

You are already amazing! Knowing this about yourself is embracing the power within. When you recognize just how amazing you are, it is then you are able to share your inner gifts with those around you. Below are just a few of these truly special gifts that you can celebrate about yourself. Do you recognize some of these wonderful qualities?

1. Listener- You are the one who lends an ear when others need to talk.

2. Caretaker- The will to help those in need. Caring for your pets. Lending a hand.

3. Honest- When your words and actions come from your heart.

4. Patient- Being calm while knowing your time will come.

5. Trustworthy- You are the one others can rely on knowing with you, all is safe.

6. Caring- Showing kindness and concern for others.

7. Kind- Showing your best self in all situations.

8. Appreciative- Always giving thanks for each day and everything in it.

9. Forgiving-Your ability to hold no grudges, rather release and let things go.

10. Charitable-Giving to others because you see a need.

Now Is Your Power

There is a very important fact about where your power is.

If we are going to find it, then we will need to look in the right place for it.

It isn't in yesterday, that has passed. It isn't in tomorrow, that hasn't come.

The one and only place you will ever find your power is NOW. How do we

find our "Now Power?"

One way is by doing mindful practices that bring you to your present

moment. It is here in this space where you will find creativity, inspiration

and empowerment in its most purest form. It is from this space where your

creative thoughts can become real things as thought is where it all begins.

Let's use this practice daily to create the most positive thoughts we can.

This brings good energy and happiness into your everyday living.

What you will need for this exercise.

A seashell and a comfortable place to sit.

When you are ready, put your seashell up to your ear, (this helps with

concentration and focus) and close your eyes while someone reads,

"Colors of the Rainbow."

Rainbow

It's time to rest so take a breath, now blow it out with ease,

As you sit quite comfortably and feel a gentle breeze.

Imagine now that you are up upon the clouds so warm,

As you gaze into the sky a rainbow starts to form.

The beauty of its colors are so beautiful and bright,

It's hard to look away from all its mesmerizing light.

The colors of the rainbow have a power and it's known,

That each one has a meaning and a gift for you to own.

Love and inspiration is that spark found deep inside,

All is there for you to use let passion be your guide.

Breathe in all the colors of the rainbow power light,

Exhale slow while feeling inspiration and delight.

Every time you see the rainbows beauty from above,

Remember you have rainbow light inside that's full of love.

Seashell's have their power

from all they left behind,

Once full of the ocean's life

in each, one of a kind

Listen very closely
as you hold close to your ear
The whispers of the seashell's past
is likely what you'll hear

Building Power Through Kindness

Love

♡ ♡

you're Amazing

Smile

Life is Good

Finding your **superhero** within is a task you can acheive simply by **giving** to others. This is an act of selflessness. When you put **yourself** in a position where you can do someting for someone **else**, you are creating **strength** through gratitude, appreciation and **thoughtfulness**. Others feel this in the receiving of it, as you will in the **giving** of it. What do you **think** this does to those who are receiving? It encourages others to **want** to do the same. Let's see what we can do to **spread** some kindness using the kindness cards.

What you will need:

1. Index cards

2. Colored pens or pencils

3. Your imagination

On one side, write a word, phrase or draw a picture of anything you think may make someone happy.

On the other side, write "Pass this on." Keep your cards with you and pass them out to people you see where ever you go.

This is how the "ripple" begins. From you, to the next person, who then passes it to the next, and on it goes!

Your card may just reach people clear across the country!

This is powerful and it all begins with you!

When being kind to others
They'll share this kindness too,
The ripple will continue
And it all begins with you.

Expression Stones

Emotions are not always easy to put into words. Sometimes we lash out when we are mad, fight when we are angry or scream when we just don't know what else to do. The good news is there are things we can do to better understand our feelings and how to express them in a more effective and positive way. When we learn how to connect our thoughts with our emotions, we create balance between the two. We learn new ways to communicate our feelings while acknowledging them fully. This enables us to respond in a more constructive and positive way. Let's bring out our inner power "warrior" by using this activity to see how we can learn to balance out our feelings and emotions.

You will need;

6 smooth palm sized stones and colored sharpies or acrylic paints. On each stone, draw or paint what ever you feel expresses these 6 emotions.

1. Happiness
2. Excitement
3. Peace
4. Hope
5. Anger
6. Fear

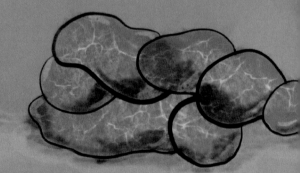

Expression Stone Activity

Each day, pick the expression stone that most closely matches up to the way you are feeling. Answer the questions and see what you might do to create a more powerful and effective thought demonstrating your emotions in a more positive way.

1. Happiness - What makes you happy? When feeling happy and full of joy, how do you think this looks to others?

2. Excitement - What do you get excited about? How do you react when you feel excited?

3. Peace - What gives you peace? Is this a good and positive emotion? What is one thing you do when you feel peaceful?

4. Hope - Do you feel hopeful at times? What makes you feel hope?

5. Anger - What do you get angry over? How do you react when you feel angry? What can you do to make your angry emotions feel more hopeful, or peaceful?

6. Fear - What do you fear most? What would you have to do to turn that fear into a more peaceful feeling?

It is always good to stay in tune with the way you feel, and why you feel this way. Being able to bring a positive response instead of lashing out in rage gives you the power and the balance to create more joy each and every day. The more you use this activity, the better you will be at discovering the best way to express your emotions.

Talk about emotions
express them every day,
You have the power to allow
new thoughts to lead the way.

Knowledge is Power

How would you find answers if you didn't ask the questions? Become a super power learner by asking questions. Ask away, raise your hand, write your questions, read lots of books, ask teachers, parents and others and get your answers to become a Superhero of Knowledge. All of us are learners as well as teachers. What we learn we can then share with others. Today you may be the learner, and tomorrow you may be the teacher. Being knowledgeable helps our confidence, self- esteem and helps us become self-reliant.

Now, use your resources and find the answers to these five popular questions. Then, ask some questions that you would like the answers to.

1. Why is the sky blue?
2. .Why do ladybugs have spots?
3. Why did dinosaurs go extinct?
4. Why do I need to eat vegetables?
5. Where does a rainbow end?

Fitness Power

Give your Inner Superhero the strength it needs by providing your physical body with the activities it takes to develop firm muscles, strong bones and good heart health. Just minutes each day can boost your energy levels, improve posture, increase physical wellness and promote emotional growth. You can make exercising fun by creating new activities that get your body moving. Attempt these playful exercises. Then try inventing your own games and challenges.

Let's begin with some hula hoop fun!

1. Classic Spin - Spin the hoop around your waist and see how long you can keep spinning. Add another hoop to increase your coordination.

2. Pass the Hoop - Have a group form a circle and hold hands. Ask two people to let go of their grip long enough to place their hands through a hoop, then rejoin hands. The task is to pass the hoop around the circle until it returns to the starting point. You may step through the hoop, use your body and arms. Get creative!

3. Hoop Jump - Like a jump rope, hold the hoop vertically in front of your body. Flip it down toward your feet, jump and bring it over behind your head and jump again and again.

4. Arm Spins - Spin your hoop by placing it on one arm, making it go around and around. Now try two. One on each arm.

5. Hoop Scotch - With several hoops, make a pattern on the ground and skip through them. Try and not land on the hoops.

Power Balls

Make your own power snack before or after exercising to fuel your body.

2 cups oats

1/2 cup raw honey

1/2 cup mini chocolate chips

1 cup extra crunchy peanut butter or almond butter

1/2 cup sunflower seeds

2 tbs flax seed

In food processor, pulse all ingredients until fully combined

Make tablespoon sized balls

Put on wax papered cookie sheet

Put in fridge for 2 hrs.

130 calories each

* For those with peanut allergies, Sunflower seed butter may be subsituted.

Be the best that you can be
through food and exercise,
Build your body and your mind
be powerful and wise.

Power of Love

Love is the most powerful emotion known to humankind. Think about it. When you feel love, it is amazing! It fills your heart with joy in a way nothing else can. Have you ever experienced love for a new kitten or puppy?

Maybe a new baby brother or sister? Love is so powerful and it is living right inside of you. It is from this place inside, you can share your love with others. Loving yourself and loving others creates support, self-esteem and a belief in oneself. Love helps you grow and flourish into strong confident beings. So let's support ourselves and others by accepting and giving love.

Using small square pieces of paper, write 30 special sayings, notes, or actions to do. Example, Hug your pet, write a special note to your best friend, call and tell your grandparents you are thinking of them, etc. Put all the notes in an envelope. Hang the envelope on your fridge so you can pull out one note per day for 30 days. This will be your Love task for the day. This practice is just a fun reminder to do something in a loving way each day. You're not only filling your heart, but you are filling others with joy and happiness and love as well.
This is Your Power of Love.

Love

Love Notes

Power Achiever

Setting goals and challenges is a great way to boost confidence while feeling a sense of pride and self-esteem. Achieving your goals and challenges can help your inner power feel the success in all the wonderful things you set out to do. Your ambitions become strong, motivation is unstoppable and daily life takes on more meaning. Great things are accomplished when you believe you can. One way to help you keep track and see what progress you have made is by creating your very own Accomplishment Box.

For this project you will need:

1. Empty tissue box

2. Glue or tape

3. Color crayons, pens or paints

4. Construction paper

5. Your imagination

Now the fun begins! Each day, write down one thing you did that feels like an accomplishment to you. This could be as simple as going outside and appreciating the beauty in your yard, helping someone out, finishing your chores, etc. Once you have written your accomplishment down, drop it into your box. At the end of each month, take out your accomplishments and go over all the wonderful things you achieved.

You are a Super Power Achiever!

Accomplish one thing everyday set goals and then believe,
That confidence and self-esteem is what you will achieve.

Cut your construction paper into squares to fit the sides of your box. Decorate the squares how ever you'd like and glue or tape onto your new Accomplishment Box.

Power of the Universe

The Universe is one massive endless space of power and you are a part of it. Imagine that! You are a speck upon this planet, this planet is a speck within this solar system, the solar system is a speck in this galaxy and this galaxy is a speck within the Universe. That is super power! When you use your imagination, you are using the power this Universe offers. Your imagination is limitless just like all the space around you. When you believe you can be, do and have what ever it is you desire, it is first created in your imagination. Let's use our imagination by gazing into the night sky.

When night has come and chores are done, it's time to go out and gaze into the night. Find a place where you can lay down comfortably, maybe a trampoline, on the grass or a loung chair. Now the fun begins. Imagine you are a beem of light, streaming rapidly up into space. Past the moon, beyond the stars and into the vast darkness of space. Use your imagination to create a story. It is here where you can be as adventurous as you like. There are no boundries in this space. What do you see? Can you sense cool air or heat? Can you reach out and touch or grab anything? Is there noise or silence? When you are done with your night gazing, get your drawing materials. Now draw all you saw while you were way up above the stars. You are the creator of your own story. Do this execise several times each week.

Look into the midnight sky
Beyond the stars so bright.
As this is where your thoughts create
Inspiring delight.

Clean Clutter, Create Brain Power!

Messy rooms happen! It may not be the most exciting thing to clean up all that clutter from the floors, dresser and bed yet there are reasons why you should.

Clearing out the clutter from your personal space actually helps bring clarity, thought and focus to your brain. Outer clutter, creates inner chaos. Making your space free from all the "stuff" opens up your mind space, giving you the power to feel more inspired, alert and strengthens emotional balance. Make your space a comfortable and relaxing place just for you! Once you do, prepare a special spot. Call it your retreat, sanctuary or zen den. You might want to put a big cushion or beanbag chair in your new space. To make your space even better, add a diffuser. Dropping some wonderful oils into your diffuser will help uplift your mood while filling the air with new fresh scents. So, let's get started and clear that clutter, relax and take a deep breath.

Clean room, Clear mind.

By doing daily practices imagine what you'll find,

The superhero deep inside is you one of a kind.

When looking for your power, remember what is true,

You never have to look too far, this power lies in you.

I Found My Power!

I Found

My Power!

I Found

My Power!

I Found My Power!

I Found My Power!

About the Author

Patricia May became an author writing children's books in 2015. After attending several Hay House conventions, Patricia was inspired to teach children the wonderful methods and practices she had learned and carried with her throughout her life. Creating and writing these books are her passion. Encouraging children to develope a life of peace and harmony is her goal.

Patricia has been honored to have many of her books endorsed by Hay House authors, teachers and speakers who inspired her through her spiritual journey. As she has been encouraged to share her teachings, she now motivates others to do the same.

Patricia lives in the gorgeous foothills of Amador County with her supportive husband, her poodles, and all her kids and grandkids living close by.

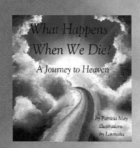